Unwillingly Yours
By
D. M. Palmer

Acknowledgement

I would like to take the time to dedicate this book to my best friend, confidante and sister in Christ!   We have spent time together through good and bad but we continue to hold each other up. Thank you, Judy, for your love and encouragement over the years. I want to, also, recognize my husband, my family and my friends for the trust and confidence they have in me. Awe-Some!

DISCLAIMER

INTRODUCTION

We live in an amazing world full of many opportunities, careers, lifestyles and types and forms of educations. I don't believe anyone can deny that we, as Americans, can and do utilize these things everyday through many generations. To be able to have that hope for our selves as well as our children is very encouraging.

Through the years I have worked, raised my children, paid my bills, dreamed for the future and planned for retirement just like each and every one of you. In my youth, however, I lived in a bit of a fantasy world. You know, the white picket fences and rosy futures with no problems with life, relationships, transportation and money. When reality hits it hits hard! There's never enough money to go around so you begin the " chase your tail" routine. What do you do? How do you generate more money without taking time away from your children? Is there always going to be more bills in the mail- box than what is going into your bank account? Maybe yes, maybe no. That's the concern we all will face sooner or later.

Working hard and doing the best we know how may not be enough for many Americans. The more income one makes the higher the tax bracket you will find yourself in and the more you will pay into the government out of the monies you worked for. This doesn't seem to be the fairest condition that we all have to face each and every year. Take a good look at your payroll stub then ask yourself if there is anything you could be doing with the amount that is being taken out for state and federal taxes. If you can say you really couldn't use it then, I believe you would be quite a minority.

My frustration over paying taxes, as we are required to do, has culminated into this book. I want to make it clear, however, that I do realize that our government does require money to finance the operations of a large government as ours. I do not agree with how they are collected nor how the IRS has the ability to destroy the lives of those who struggle to pay taxes.

The general public has no clue as to how their tax dollars are being used or misused. We don't know who has the power to spend our tax dollars nor do we have the ability to say whether we want to pay taxes at all. Congress voted in the taxing system (IRS) after the Supreme Court said it was "unconstitutional". Does that surprise you? I wasn't a bit surprised by that little bit of historical information!

"My fellow American's" as President Kennedy would say, if you have similar concerns and question the practices, powers and principles of the IRS read the rest of this book with an open mind. When you are finished consider what you can do to effect a change in how our system concerning taxes and the collection of said monies.

Chapter One

Today, we American's live in an ever-changing system. When we wake in the mornings our lives can change drastically without desire or notice. Our homes, jobs, family and more are at risk! Our very livelihood cannot be controlled or manipulated by our own hands but, can and are by the government that runs this country.

Hard working people try to live the American dream each and every day with hopes of those dreams coming true. Some try as they may, never reach their goals and grow old with very little more than they started their lives with. A few may reach some financial success and others only reach a level that make others envy or loathe them. There is a lot of low and middle class Americans that could be much more successful if there was a little more money in their pockets. Failure to achieve a better way of life for our families and us is directly related to our economy and all the forces behind it. It's bad enough that every consumable item in this country is so expensive that most people have to juggle their income to cover the expenses of everyday life. I don't need to tell you that gasoline; groceries, insurance, clothing, personal hygiene items, housing, furnishing, transportation, childcare, education and many more items are an everyday concern.

In many households, parents of children must both maintain steady gainful employment in order to stay afloat. Should one or the other become sick or injured for any length of time any possession or progress they have acquired may disappear before their eyes. Sound familiar? Could this happen to you? Are there any measures you can take to guard against such a tragedy? Maybe.

The daily news, no mater which media you care to watch, are not going to be able to give you the "rest of the story" as Paul Harvey would say. I realize that we all are not politically inclined but it doesn't take a scholar to know when our hard earned monies are being abused and done so without our knowledge. You most likely will hear of the shootings, abductions, rapes, robberies and every other thing going on throughout our country but not what's happening with our money. When I hear of these broadcasts I don't have to wonder why they happen because it's easy to realize when the people of this country are pushed to their limits! A good portion of the crime statistics is associated to the monetary condition of those involved.

Many Americans would do anything to live in better areas, buy a better or bigger home or improve their lifestyle if they had the means to do so but finances prohibit any and possibly all progress. Some become physically ill due to lack of adequate foods, some will suffer stress or depression to the extent of mental illness resulting in suicide and some are forced to rely on our welfare system or homelessness. These are the times we all live in!

I am sure that all of you would change something in your life if it were feasible to do so. This is why I want each of you to realize that I have concentrated on one entity in this book that could possibly change many lives without it's existence.

Not all agencies, groups or services are beneficial, as they appear to be. Surprise! Have you had this experience with any government agencies that you thought was there for the purposes that you were in need of?

Try working with the IRS when you find yourself in need of an extension. There will be a process involved and penalties to pay before it's all done! Fair? Maybe not but that's their rules that we all are faced with.

Can't pay the amount that is due at the end of the year according to your 1040? Anyone can arrange a payment plan but here is where the shock fits in. Penalties and interest will be assessed to the unpaid balance for as long as it takes you to pay your debt. Decide not to pay at all and your life may be taking on a whole different look! Jail may be in your future.

Should we have to live through the stress and fear that is a constant part of the dark side of the IRS that we are supporting? I am, personally saddened and ashamed that our country allows this practice to continue against the hard working people in America! Many have given their lives for this country out of their love of it and, yet, it's not enough! Americans are supporting this land NOT the politicians in Washington. They are our employees and it's time we are respected for our position! Anyone have a similar view? If you haven't yet, read on maybe that will change. If you do, you may enjoy the rest of this story.

Chapter Two

The history of the Internal Revenue Service takes us as far back as the Civil War. President Lincoln, in 1862, had asked our Congress to create a job position named "Commissioner of Internal Revenue. At the very same time, President Lincoln would enact an income tax designed to pay the expenses of the war. This event would mark the first time an income tax had been charged to the people of America.

After ten years had passed, the tax would be repealed. The war had been over for several years, the war had been paid for and the tax was no longer a necessity.

Americans must have been thrilled not to be required to keep paying these taxes even though they must have been very passionate about this country!

Though the Civil War was over and had been for years the foundations had been laid for taxes in America. This would mean that the IRS would not stay dead.

This country was facing a gigantic debt in1894 and a new income tax was viewed as a very easy way to rid us of this problem. A perfect picture came into view for Congress later that year which seemed to be an easy fix to their debt problem. Congress would bring the income tax back to life just to be shot down by the Supreme Court who quickly ruled it unconstitutional. " Specifically, the 1894 income tax failed to meet the constitutional requirement that laws be charged proportionally by population." Because of this the income tax disappeared for almost twenty years.

People of America, this should mean something today! We have a Constitution for a reason and our Fore Fathers made sure we all were protected from many wrongs. We must not ignore our rights according to this established document, The Constitution of America!

Since the income tax was unconstitutional in 1894, Congress would believe the best way to fix the problem they had with debt was to change our constitution. With the help of Woodrow Wilson ratifying the 16th amendment, that's exactly what they did. When the 16t amendment was ratified it gave Congress authority to enact an income tax on the American people.

This new amendment carried a lot of weight in it's wording. I will include the most important part of this amendment: "Congress shall have the power to lay and collect taxes on incomes, from whatever source derived, without apportionment among the several states without regard to any census or enumeration."

Ratifying the amendment, Wyoming gets credit for being the state for doing so. With a three-quarter majority, which was needed to ratify this amendment, Wyoming would be the 36th and final state to amend the Constitution.

As time went by, Congress would create a 1% tax on all net personal incomes above $3,000, including 6% surtax on incomes higher than $500,000. These rates may not sound like much to us today. Due to inflation, however, less than 10% of Americans, at that time, were affected by the tax.

Though the Internal Revenue Service would not be referred to as such for decades, Americans would file their first 1040 Form in 1913 for the first time in the history of this country. Due to this reason our government established the Bureau of Internal Revenue.

The US would ratify another amendment to our constitution in 1919. This would be the 18th Amendment, which would ban the sale of alcohol across the United States. Because of this we would now, officially, have entered the Prohibition era.

Since we were involved in this era, Congress decided to pass the Volstead Act, which gave the Commissioner of Internal Revenue the main responsibility of reinforcing Prohibition.

That responsibility would be passed to the Department of Justice some eleven years later. It is an important note that the IRS had once enforced Prohibition in the organization's history. One important fact to come from the IRS during Prohibition is one most of us have heard of. It is well known of the charges brought against Al Capone for tax evasion. The IRS had assigned their Intelligence Unit agent to Capone's case, which led to him spending 11 years in prison on those charges.

Prohibition was repealed in 1933 and in 1934 the IRS took on a new responsibility of taxation of alcohol. They were also, given the duties of administering the National Firearms Act. After this, they were given the task of enforcing the taxes on tobacco. Imagine the power they had then, much less now! I was under the impression that the IRS represented the position of a clearinghouse for our tax dollars so the money could be distributed accordingly. I have been very wrong on this issue and I believe many Americans have no real concept as to what they do or how they really operate. Isn't it time we all know what is being done with our money, how it's being acquired and what measures our Government will go to dip into our pockets?

By 1942, President Roosevelt would face the rising costs of World War II. At this time, The Revenue Act would be passed to help with these costs and it would be called "the greatest tax bill in American history". This bill would pass through Congress and it would "change the way Americans viewed taxes to this day".

Roosevelt's Revenue Act not only changed the amount of taxes we would pay, but it increased the number of Americans who had to pay income taxes. This Act would create allowable deductions for medical and investment expense

By the end of World War II, Congress had began new features such as, payroll withholding and quarterly tax installments as a part of the Current Tax Payment Act of 1943 and The Individual Income Tax Act of 1944

By the 1950's The Bureau of Internal Revenue would take on its new name of Internal Revenue Service.

During this time many things in America began changing. Our population would explode, the economy was booming and the IRS was recording record tax revenue. With these changes came the necessity for major re-organization to take care of the demands of the modernization in America.

President Truman was in office at this time and he knew that changes were needed. By 1952, he would propose the Reorganization Plan No. 1. This plan would replace the patronage system at the IRS with a new career civil service system. It was, also, meant to decentralize service to taxpayers and to restore public confidence in the service.

The final change that came during the 1950's was the filing deadline for individual tax returns. That date would be changed from March 15th to April 15th and would be effective in 1954.

From this point other changes have occurred such as, the age of computers and electronic filing. These are portrayed as an advantage to all Americans for our convenience. I am sure they have made life a lot less painful for all of us and yet, my thoughts haven't changed where this agency is concerned!

History of this nation is fascinating on so many levels. Americans have always wanted a better country to live in and to raise their families. Wars have been fought, lives have been lost, dreams have been reached and disappointment has been overcome. Should we be fighting our own government for what our Forefathers worked so hard to give us? This is something we all should ask ourselves everyday. America has a responsibility to guard the integrity of our Constitution and not let changes be made to it to make a quick fix due to poor management of our leaders.

Chapter Three

Now we have talked about the history concerning the IRS but, with all due respect, we need to discuss the negative parts that are lying in the shadows.

We have discussed the issue of the deadline of April 15th of each year. There are few exceptions to this rule and the stress of being prepared, motivated, mentally able or qualified to file all necessary forms in the proper manner may be more than anyone wants to face. The deadline is only the beginning of this nightmare!

What would happen if you couldn't file on time, you owe and can't pay, you haven't filed in years or you have had other issues concerning your income tax requirements? If you have the issue of non-payment you may have a small incite into the extent that the IRS will take.

Here is where penalties and punishment seem to fly out of control. The investigation into these issues is astounding and not what Americans should have to face from their government agencies.

We all have taxes removed from our payroll checks when we are employed for someone and if you are self-employed you will be required to pay in on a determined schedule. Either way Americans will be paying income taxes accordingly. Congress, as you may remember, saw fit that taxes would no longer be only used for one debt but for many others. No longer would there be an end to taxes and the penalties and interest that they charge on unpaid taxes can grow to unbelievable amounts.

Let's assume you are and average American that is struggling raising a family, working an average job, making a house payment with the normal expenses involved in maintaining that and saving a little on the side. Each week a payroll check is paid to you and the normal tax deductions are removed before you get that check whether you like it or not. During the year the question enters your mind of "what if those taxes were Not removed"? Could you have used them?

The year comes to an end and it's time to consider preparing for tax time. The hope of a refund is there but you could owe more taxes. Checking all your paper work and the deductions available to you according to the tax laws for that year you begin. Hours later the bad news will hit like running into a brick wall at sixty miles an hour. You owe more taxes!

With your head in your hands, stomach churning, mind reeling and fear growing you know you don't have enough money to pay this debt. Do you file or not? The IRS says "yes", money or not.

Let's start here with the idea of filing without payment. The Internal Revenue Service will gladly set you up on a payment plan for a fee. The penalty is much less if you do file but don't pay your taxes. The IRS will charge you a 0.5% of your unpaid debt for each month that you don't pay up to 25%. One must remember, however, that interest will accrue on all unpaid taxes. The interest rate is equal to the "federal short-term rate" plus 3%.

Should you decide not to file at all, the penalty will be 5% of the unpaid amount for each month your tax return is late up to 25%. In addition, if you should file more tan 60 days late, you will be required to pay a minimum of $135 or 100% of the taxes you owe (whichever is less).

People, this is not where this ends! Not only can the IRS dig into your pockets during the year they can charge outrageous amounts of money in penalties and interest on a debt that you are struggling with already.

If you choose to ignore this concerning income tax debt the punishment will become much worse. The IRS can and will file a notice of a federal tax lien, meaning they can lay claim to your property. Should they seize the house or other property you own, the IRS will sell the interest that you own in the property and apply those proceeds to your tax debt. Before selling your property they will calculate a minimum bid price and provide you with a copy of that calculation. At that time they will give you the opportunity to challenge the fair market value determination. After this is done, the IRS will provide you with the notice of sale and make the sale known to the public through local newspapers, flyers or public places. The proceeds from the sale will pay for the cost of seizing and selling the property and, of course, your tax debt. Should there be any proceeds left over after your debt is paid, the IRS will let you know how to receive a refund.

This isn't much of a consequence after losing your home or all that you felt you worked for in your life but this is another penalty you may face.

Ignoring the situation further can lead to felony charges of tax evasion, which is punishable by imprisonment. This would demonstrate a willful attempt to defraud.

I don't believe any American should have this to worry about nor is it my belief than this type of condition should exist in this country. When Congress saw fit to by pass the Supreme Court and change the constitution it would become inevitable for the powers of the IRS to become as they are.

The destruction of American lives is the image that comes to mind for me in these type of situations. When a family is faced with losing the home they have lived in, their livelihood and the dispersal of the family unit that is a catastrophe!   To fear this in this country is beyond understanding.

Americans are faced with this very thing. If not jail time, financial destruction can end many lives all because a debt could not be paid. There are several states that can place a person in jail just for the non-payment of a debt. The IRS is not the only one but the suffering is the same.

Chapter Four

We now know that we can be subject to punishment by the IRS of federal tax liens, seizure of our property, forfeiture of refunds, tax evasion charges and revocation of your passport. Punishment has played a role in all our lives at one point or another for many reasons. As a child we were punished for miss behaving, not coming home on time or talking back to our parents. When we violate the rules of the road a ticket is in our future. Should we step past the established laws in this country and commit a felony a prison sentence will be handed down. Punishment has it's place and rightfully so. No one should be above the law nor should we be made criminals in order to fit the guidelines of the law.

The 13th Amendment of our Constitution states: "Neither slavery nor involuntary servitude, except as a punishment for crime whereof the party shall have been duly convicted, shall exist within the United States, nor any place subject to their jurisdiction." This Amendment was ratified on December 6, 1865. This particular amendment is interesting on so many levels. The wording of "involuntary servitude" jumps off the page when it comes to many ways of our government but especially when it comes to the IRS and income taxes.

Let's take a look at our status in this country as taxpayers. Throughout history congress and the sitting president have decided that Americans would be paying income taxes. This was not a choice given to the people of America. Does that fit into the "involuntary servitude" definition?

When taxes are removed from your wages before your payroll check is given to you does that fit the "involuntary servitude" definition? When you are required to work overtime and more taxes are withdrawn would you consider this a part of the "involuntary servitude" definition? America is required to obey the established laws but what happens when our rights are violated? Can we depend on the same laws to protect us or are those laws only interpreted one way. Congress haste ability to have our constitution changed to suit its need so how do we.

As Americans fight that? In my personal opinion I believe that our government representatives have forgotten who works for whom. In this country the American people are the employers of those representing us in Washington. Under no circumstances does an employee have the right to make the rules without the approval of management. Many things happen in Washington that are not brought to the attention of the taxpayers nor are they a part of the decision to approve or disapprove an article of choice. As Americans we must stand up for what we believe to be the rights given to all of us. I am sure we would all agree that it takes a lot of money to run this massive county but not at the expense of the lives of the innocent. Here is where the collection of taxes becomes a major eye sore and an embarrassment to me. There are many different views where income taxes and the collection thereof are concerned. In my personal view I see extortion, violation of my constitutional rights, intimidation, and wrongful loss of property and destruction of human life.

When we have to fear penalties for not filing on time or not being able to pay more taxes that becomes a big fault with our system. Americans are not the cash cow that our government seems to think we are. America represents the best of the best to the whole world and we should be proud to live in such a place.

The best part of living here is that change is always welcome but there is still darkness that needs light. Our own government brought light to the families of organized crime around our country for our betterment. In doing so they exposed many crimes that would bring prison sentences to some well-known individuals for tax evasion to murder.

Is America better for the curb on organized crime? Of course we are. We would be fools to believe otherwise however; maybe some of those very same practices are still alive and well today. Illegal or legal? Does it depend on who is using the practices?

Chapter Five

Organized crime thrives on supplying illegal goods and services for which a large number of people are willing to pay. These groups have a goal of making money and their members gain a sense of pride, power and protection. Organized crime groups operate in a pyramid power structure like legal business. Members of these groups are fiercely loyal and committed. Punishment for members who choose to stray can be demoted to a lower rank or, depending on the offense, death. Why would anyone get involved with such business with the knowledge of the consequences of the wrong choices? Could money play such an important role that a person would be willing to take chances with their very lives?

For many years we have heard the stories of many of the organized crime families and their practices. Al Capone to John Gotti brought news of charges of racketeering, hijacking, loan sharking, drug trafficking, bookmaking, prostitution, extortion, pornography, illegal gambling and many other criminal activities. In 1992, John Gotti was convicted of five murders, conspiracy to commit murder, racketeering, obstruction of justice, tax evasion, illegal gambling, extortion and loan sharking. From these charges he was convicted and sentenced to life without parole.

Anyone that is convicted of any or all of these crimes should be subject to the same prison sentence. America has established laws for this very reason. We as citizens cannot allow our streets to be corrupted or used illegally for anyone's financial gain or power status. In the old days of organized crime people were being gunned down on the streets and innocent by-standers were sometime victims of those incidents. These had to be frightening times. When a crime boss handed down punishment it would be swift and final.

What does all of this have to do with the IRS? The obvious would be the tax evasion involved by the business practices of organized crime groups but there is a bit more to look at in the operations of both.

Let's take a look at the word "extortion". According to the dictionary the definition is "the practice of obtaining something, especially money, through force or threats". According to Find law, most states define extortion "as the gaining of property or money by almost any kind of force or threat or violence, property damage, harm to reputation, or unfavorable government action...". Extortion, as a crime is punishable as a felony offense in most states and federal law.

Why would this be important to any of us as taxpayers? Our government does not allow even organized crime groups to get away with extortion without consequences and yet we American's are allowing the IRS to do it unfettered. When Congress decided to go above the Supreme Court's decision that income taxes were unconstitutional and changed the 16th amendment of the constitution to make taxing legal "extortion" became legal. Of course, this legality would only apply to one entity, exclusively. This view may not be held by all but I am sure that there are many Americans who would prefer that the IRS kept their hands out of their pockets.

How is collection of income taxes extortion? Every working person is required to pay these taxes and at the rate that has been established by their offices. We have deadlines to file our yearly tax forms with threat of punishment. If one owes you had better pay, if one is due a refund, you will wait. There will always be penalties for late payment or nonpayment and no interest on refunds.

Extortion? Legal or illegal? How would you view the evidence so far? We as Americans have the right to answers And should not allow our government to change our constitution to use against us.

Let's take a look at another term that fits between these two groups. Tax evasion is a term that can be used quite loosely and without much truth behind it. According to the definition of Investopedia tax evasion is "an illegal activity in which a person or entity deliberately avoids paying a true tax liability. Those caught evading taxes are generally subject to criminal charges and substantial penalties. To willfully fail to pay taxes is a federal offense under the Internal Revenue Service tax code."

Punishment for tax evasion can be imprisonment for no more than 5 years, a fine of not more than $250,000 for individuals or $500,000 for corporations or both plus the cost involved in the prosecution there of.

In view of what we have learned so far how can tax evasion exist knowing that it's possible that our income taxes are taken wrongfully to begin with? Just because the Congress changes an amendment of our constitution should not validate a criminal act. America we cannot commit a crime if one doesn't exist! People in this country work hard to raise their families and should not have to live in fear for their very lives.

Crime bosses around the world have plenty examples to operate by or maybe it's the other way around. We don't have the IRS having gun fights in the streets but they do know how to get their man. The difference is the swift and final death verses the slow financial torture that comes with tax penalties and fines.

Real crime does exist in this country without the average American becoming a criminal because of lack of resources. Many may be guilty of poor financial management but that doesn't rise to the level of criminal action due to it. Our representatives in Washington can't manage money any better or balance a budget so why are we expected to do so.

As you can see, "tax evasion" can be used quite loosely and not quite as accurate as it should be. By definition it is the "willful failure to pay taxes" which does not fit the parameters of many cases. There are Americans who struggle to do the right thing and just can't seem to get ahead of the system. Rules, regulations and deadlines do not coincide with the availability of their finances. Complying seems to be an impossible task without the situation snowballing before your eyes.

Will the next step be an accusation of tax evasion? What then?

These days there are resources to turn to for help with tax debt all over the country. The sad thought is that we will need them at all. Agencies making money off the broken backs of the American taxpayer may be the American way but, a solution to something we shouldn't have to have.

Chapter Six

Many laws have been established in this land to protect its citizens and we should be thankful for them. However, those laws don't always apply to all. One of those laws was established to guard against racketeering, generally associated with organized crime in this country. Investopedia defines racketeering as "crimes committed through extortion or coercion." This definition brings to mind the idea of the 13th amendment of involuntary servitude. How you ask? Income tax payments! The IRS can remove money from income earned by any American by their established law which was originally unconstitutional. That's not by choice, that's involuntary servitude, which violates the 13th amendment. With that removal of money comes another violation of extortion due to the threats if that liability is not paid and then, the final straw is racketeering because this practice is being done repeatedly. Illegal is not what the establishment would call it. Congress went to great lengths to legalize extortion, coercion, racketeering and involuntary servitude just to meet their needs.

Upon doing research one will find that most all of these crimes are associated with organized crime operations. RICO, which stands for the "Racketeer Influenced and Corrupt Organizations act", passed into law in 1970 in response to a serious problem with organized crime in the United States. This new act would make a big difference concerning the operations of these organized crime groups but would only be concerned with those. If a crime is being committed then our laws should apply to all. Strangely enough that's not the case. We as citizens and taxpayers of this great country seemingly have no influence in these matters as we should have. Many of the laws that have been established can and are used against the very same people that they were meant to protect.

When is a crime a crime and does it matter who commits the crime in order to be prosecuted for that crime? The IRS is not above the law as is any other person or group.

The definitions given here are not mine but those of others or institutions. Ignorance in how extortion, coercion, racketeering, involuntary servitude and tax evasion are viewed is the hope of our government. I am sure that they bank on the fact that they hold the power to get what they want. When Congress made the decision to change our constitution they would create a lifetime of questions for future generations to come.

We are guilty of aiding in their acts of possible crime throughout the years. The American people should have never allowed the changing of our constitution in the first place. The Supreme Court was correct in their initial ruling and that should have been the end of the matter but Congress wanted more. By having the 16th amendment changed they got what they wanted and we were on the hook as the cash cow.

Income taxes are not the only way to support this country! Punishment, from interest and fines to imprisonment is beyond comprehension. Americans don't receive interest for the use of their money during the year that they overpay so, how dare our government bill for interest they say we owe on taxes due.

According to the 8th Amendment, "Excessive bail shall not be required, nor excessive fines imposed, nor cruel and unusual punishments inflicted", the people of this country should be able to stand strong against the procedures of the IRS. When the American Constitution was written it was to have purpose for all of us and for every generation to come. It's not just another piece of paper to be ignored or used as a last resort. It wasn't to be changed to suit Congress for whatever the reason they have in mind nor was it just a part of our history

Chapter Seven

The whole idea of an income tax is and always has been unconstitutional. If we are to believe and trust in our government then we need our representatives fighting for us, not against us. Every elected official works for the people not the other way around yet, the roles are apparently not as they should be. Why would anyone run for any office? Is the heart of that individual true to the people's needs and desires or are their eyes on power and money to line their own pockets? We all take that chance by electing an individual to an office. Corruption is everywhere and not as visually prominent as we would like. Our government goes to great length to make us aware of the Organized Crime Families and their faults and punishments but, not of their own. Many times the blame of an incident will be laid on another's back to take the heat off the one who should be subject to the punishment. A general cover up begins and snowballs until no one can see the truth. I am, personally, ashamed of myself for not being more active in making my American a better place. A single person can and has changed the futures of many.

Looking back in our own history demonstrates the accuracy in how changes occur and affect so many of us, even today. When our ancestors arrived in this land so long ago, they were looking for religious freedom and a way of life that they had a say so in. People of America have struggled against rulers and unjust systems for many generations and will continue long after my generation is gone. With growing population and modernization brings necessary change but the basis of human desire will never be different.

The belief that one or a few have the right to speak for all Americans is ridiculous. A fine example of this would be that of Madalyn Murray O'Hair who was an "American activist supporting atheism and separation of church and state". She was the founder of the American Atheists in 1963 and served as the organizations president until 1986.

This woman was heard around the world for her views on many religious matters. One, single woman was able to change the view of our courthouses, federal buildings, schools and much more by her voice alone. The 10 Commandments that had been displayed on the walls of public buildings would be withdrawn, prayer and the Pledge of Allegiance were no longer allowed in our schools and much more of the like would become a thing of history.

In America we have many diverse religions, lifestyles and ethnic groups that we are to respect for what they are. How is it that this one woman can change so much for so many? If you were to look at her methods to achieve all that she did you will find she used bullying, foul language, consistency and her rights under the constitution as an American citizen. She pushed her beliefs to the limit, this is true, but she accomplished much in her time in the limelight.

As you can see, making changes in our world doesn't take an army it takes determination. We all can make a difference in this land for ourselves if we try. I don't suggest using Madalyn's methods but a heartfelt determination would go a long way. In my opinion, I don't believe she had respect for anyone for any reason but she was very headstrong in accomplishing her goals.

Respect is quite necessary to live in this world and that's not an overused quality of many Americans of today. The lack of respect brings about issues that involve us in the political problems that will drag us down whether we want it to or not. That is an issue that does need to change for all else to mend. Power given to a few will not and never has been the answer.

Changes are meant to be making a situation better however this isn't always true. The changes that were made due Madalyn Murray O'Hair's efforts didn't make all Americans happy. Her views had been pushed on the rest of the world whether they agreed or not. I'll guarantee you that only a select few were satisfied with the results of her efforts.

Who stood against her in the system? It's evident that not many voiced their beliefs or rights against her because she was able to get what she wanted and it's still evident today.

When our Congress went beyond the Supreme Court to change the 16th Amendment to keep the IRS active for the collection of income taxes they were successful because of determination not respect. If it had been respect for the constitution as it was written and the decision of the Supreme Court the 16th Amendment would still exist as our forefathers wrote it. Not only did congress not respect our courts but also they did not respect the people of America or the generations to come. Without that precious commodity, "respect", we don't have a chance.

When the Constitution of the United States of America was written it meant life and death to those who wrote it and it has become to be known as just a historical paper. Not to me! Not to Madalyn Murray O'Hair whether she realized it or not. How about your feelings toward it?

We cannot let our representatives have the power to change the constitution for their purposes under any circumstances. They have proven by their reputations that the trust for their decisions has little merit.

Chapter Eight

Given our personal views, which are vast and wide considering the population, we see actions of others differently. Not one of us is an exception to this rule. Over the years many have debated the issue of paying income taxes being voluntary or involuntary. No matter which way they are, might they be illegal in any form? The views should be voiced and considered, however our government has made up their mind on this issue. Paying income taxes are not voluntary and they have been made sure they are legal by whatever means they choose.

Interpretation of "crime" is out of focus and nonexistent when it comes to the operations of our government. Absolute clean hands are not the pictures that come to mind concerning them to me. My opinion? You bet! We, as free Americans have our own opinions and I am sure they vary but in the end we all want the same things.

Our freedoms are important to everyone and the need to believe in them is a necessity for all. We need to depend on the laws to cover everyone the same way all of the time and those same laws to protect us when it is needed. In no way should our Constitution of the United States be allowed to be changed to fit the present needs of our politicians. Our forefathers would role over in their graves knowing what has been done to that precious document.

Many people have argued the point of income taxes being illegal and by the rules of today that theory is wrong. Our congress has made it legal to collect these taxes against our will and we don't have a leg to stand on. I honestly believe that it is still illegal because the changing of the constitution was not given to vote by the American people nor was the Supreme Court's decision respected

Why would that be important to any of us? If we are not allowed a voice in the operations of our government and their practices then they have freedom to do as they please any time they choose. Whatever our government does affects all of us one way or another. When this happens another of our freedoms is affected and it will, usually, dip into the pockets of every American.

Every time a scandal in Washington's political employees appears and a Grand Jury is needed we American's are on the hook for the cost of those hearings. Made up charges or valid we are paying the bill. As generous a country as this is, I do believe there is a limit for each of us as to how our money is being spent.

When we question the legality of paying income taxes we have that right! Elected representatives work for us and rarely we see progress being made with the American people in mind. Our politicians are wealthy and have benefits that many of us do not have. Spending money is what they do and some of that spending is quite necessary but, on the other hand, when does it go too far?

The American people need to take back what was given to them from the beginning. We are their employers not their servants. Here is where the 8th Amendment of our Constitution should reflect this by saying, "Neither slavery or involuntary servitude, except as punishment for a crime whereof the party shall have been duly convicted, shall exist within the United States, or any place subject to their jurisdiction".

We cannot allow laws to be made that hurt our families and us anymore. I believe in this country but we have put it in the hands of others that may not be in the same frame of mind. Power and money can change a person and their direction

Chapter Nine

Where do we go from here? Can we fight "city hall" as they say? Is it too late? NO! President John Kennedy once said, "It's not what your country can do for you but what you can do for your country" and this has always stuck in my head. I was a small girl of nine years of age at the time he spoke these words. How true that statement is! One person can make a difference, remember Madalyn Murray O'Hare? Though it may seem you are a solitary opinion on an issue you are going to find out that many others have the same beliefs and desires as you do.

Changing how our government operates is up to all Americans not just a few who make choices for all. Not everyone is going to be happy with every decision but the majority should always stand. The majority should never give in just to soothe those on the opposing side, either, and that's exactly the way I viewed the situation with Madalyn Murray O'Hare. Rather than putting up with her foul mouth and aggressive position she was allowed to accomplish what others have not. One woman!

Here is the other side of her stance, though. She would later be associated to the disappearance of a large sum of money from her own Atheist Organization and one of her sons and granddaughters. Later, all three would be found murdered. There is a right way to do all things and it's apparent that what happened here was not the correct way to handle changing a situation

Organized Crime fits in here too. Though they try to stay fairly quiet about their operations and are far more organized they still get what they want by the same means. These organizations have power and money to get what they want and that is why they protect it fiercely. How does any of this compare to our government or us for that matter?

Power and money does play a part in many things, as you may know, but it isn't the only method used. Secrecy, deceit and bulldogging occur more often than not. In this country we have many small groups coming forward against anything and everything from politics to religion. No one group should expect all others to agree with their views but, on the other hand, we should be able to respect those of others. When it comes to what our government does concerning the operations of this country that affects all unilaterally. We, all Americans, are the majority and can and should be involved in the operations of this country.

Trust is a precious item that is hard to come by when it comes to business, advertising, organizations and government agencies. We put our trust in our banks, in our lawyers, in our home security systems and our loved ones but we can be very disappointed on occasion by any of these. When we elect our representatives to Washington to support our needs there's a measure of trust issued to them for the job you hope they do. When that person fails to do as you expected the trust is broken and the vicious circle continues. The bottom line is that we all will pay!

Every time one party or the other doesn't get what they want and no compromise is found a new scandal comes out involving the other party members. The Grand Jury is convened and the hearings drag on to air the laundry of those participants, clean or dirty. The price tag for these hearings won't be a concern of those involved because the American taxpayer will be picking up the tab. We won't mind because it's our duty to serve our country and a good servant does what they are told. Expecting a lot out of Americans? Is this what we can expect for our hard earned money? Does this fall under the term "involuntary servitude"?

People of America our forefathers meant for us to have more than this. They had no idea that the document that they worked so hard on to protect us would be changed and used against us.

Laws are and have been established to thwart criminal activity and punishments have been set for those who cross the lines. We all want to know that we can expect a person or persons to be punished when a crime is committed against us. The view of this world would be much different if there were no rules and no penalties. If we are driving too fast receive a speeding ticket we would be subject to that offence. When someone embezzles money from another they are subject to those penalties. If a serial killer is apprehended and tried he or she would be penalized accordingly. No one individual should have to pay the debt of another.

If we allow our constitution to be tampered with by changing it's content we may be opening a Pandora's box. By changing the 16th Amendment we have given our finances over to our government to do as they wish. Americans cannot afford the abuse of our rights to continue. Our voices must be heard by those we employ in Washington and not discounted as being ignorant of the works of our government.

I believe that most Americans are concerned about what is going on around them. We all know how we are affected by the processes of government and want to have changes made. The problem is that most of the changes are costing the American people a fortune! The more money that is collected from each of us will never be enough and more will be expected. The government's ability to handle money is a joke and none of us could run our households the way our country is run and stay above water. Why are they not being held responsible for their own spending? It's not their money that's being spent it's ours.

The government's ability to handle money is a joke and none of us could run our households the way our country is run and stay above water. Why are they not being held responsible for their own spending? It's not their money that's being spent it's ours

Chapter Ten

Taxes are everywhere for every reason in this country. Not only are we required to pay income taxes but also there are taxes on the gasoline we use to the property that we own. A person can't buy a box of Kleenex without paying a tax on that item and we all are buying something every day.

In the state that I live in we have property taxes, personal property taxes, we are required to have inspections on our cars to license them which is another cost, taxes at the grocery store, taxes at the gas pump and on and on. Where does all this money go and for what? A homeowner will never really own their home because at the end of the year you will have a tax bill to pay. Now, you can choose not to pay this tax bill but after three years of not paying property taxes your property will be sold on the courthouse steps for the taxes due. How many times will a person be required to pay for their home?

In the local stores we are required to pay a tax of 8.1% of the items that we purchase and that is just outrageous. Where you live may higher or lower but the point is that we all are being robbed daily of our hard earned dollars. Who is handling all of this money? Where is it going and why?

Since Congress was able to achieve having the 16th amendment changed to collect income taxes everyone has jumped on the bandwagon and figured out away to "extort" more and more from all of us in America. Wrong or right it is being done and we all feel the effects of it. What can we do to take control of this mess that we have been sucked into? I don't have the answers but anything we do has to be progress in improvement of this situation.

Every American in this country has a right to reject the ideas and concepts of others as their own and that includes our government. Our representatives should be working for us not for themselves.own government representatives are taking advantage of that trait and using it against each and every one of us.

People of America, I want to impress upon you that I live just like many of you and hope and dream the same. We are the majority and are voices together are strong. American's are caring and generous to a fault   but our own government representatives are taking advantage of that trait and using it against each and every one of us.

Of all of the money taken in our country is facing a deficit of 22 trillion dollars. Why? Could it be because of excessive spending or mismanagement? Either way, our representatives are not trustworthy when it comes to handling our money! I know that there is other ways of generating funds for the use of operating this country and it sure isn't by forcing Americans to give up their paychecks. If our representatives were honestly for the people why aren't they exploring those options?

A true consumption tax would work just as well and be fair without the interpretation of "extortion". What would it be like just to pay taxes on what we buy verses having to file taxes every year? More money during the year to live and buy the items you have always wanted maybe? The bigger the item the bigger the tax, the more one buys the more the taxes. People buy what they can when they can and with consumption tax instead of the income tax people would be freer to buy.

This is just one example of a possibility and I am sure all of you have your own ideas of how to change this whirlpool of taxes we live in. If Congress can come up with an idea that was obviously unconstitutional according to the Supreme Court by changing the constitution we can demand that our constitution be returned to it's original form. By doing this, income taxes will no longer exist as we know them and our government will be forced to be frugal in their spending and research other forms of operating income from the American people.

Living in this great country has brought joy, respect, disappointment, patriotism and frustration. I have been here sixty-seven years and have seen several presidents in office. Many promises have been made some were done but, many were forgotten. I have seen many scandals from Washington's elite and professional courtesy applied with no true solution or punishment. I am sure there has been plenty cover up and half-truths in connection to these issues but we will never know. The one thing I am sure of is that the American people paid the bill for each and every one of these scandal investigations.

What I see in politics is a bunch of immature adults fighting over party lines versus working for the people that they were hired to represent. It's not about a party, people; it's about real American lives! Many of us have children or have already raised them and have grandchildren by this time but I don't believe that we would want our children to behave as these politicians do.

The bottom line is that we as Americans deserve respect and that's not how we are looked upon. We are and always have been "involuntary servants" nothing more nothing less. Keep working America and our government will take care of the rest. This is what they want from all of us. They will spend your tax dollars the way they choose as much as they want and if they want more they will have it. I'm not much into being that submissive and many of you aren't either. We must stand up against the evils in this world and make it a better place for all of us

Chapter Eleven

In conclusion of this book I want to thank each and every one of you who took the time to read these pages and have found something that has stirred your heart within them. I have been quite passionate about the subject of income taxes and how they are acquired from us and used by our government. Every year during tax time brings many emotions from frustration to anger and I don't believe that I am alone in these feelings. Many of my friends, relatives and neighbors go through a lot just to get their taxes done on time and still end up paying more at the end of the year. I watch the commercials shown on television about back taxes owed to the IRS and the levies they can put on a bank account, property and more. It's frightening what they have the power to do to people.

My hope in all of this is that the American people begin an active, legal and peaceful demonstration with their voices on Washington. We must demand that our representatives work for us or get out. We don't need another politician to give out lip service we need positive action in; favor of America.

I am going to continue writing the White House as I have done for a long time and I encourage each of you to do the same. I am including the address to the White House for your convenience: The White House, 1600 Pennsylvania Avenue NW, Washington, D.C., 205000.

Again, thank all of you and may your futures be blessed!

The people are the rightful masters Of both Congress, and Courts, not to overthrow the Constitution, but to overthrow the men who pervert it.
Abraham Lincoln-

www.ingramcontent.com/pod-product-compliance
Lightning Source LLC
Chambersburg PA
CBHW070326160726
47999CB00003B/1179